# Trombone Student



by Fred Weber
in collaboration with
Paul Tanner

## To The Student

This book, with the aid of a good teacher, is designed to help you become an excellent player on your instrument in a most enjoyable manner. It will take a reasonable amount of work and CAREFUL practice on your part. If you do this, learning to play should be a valuable and pleasant experience.

## To The Teacher

The Belwin "Student Instrumental Course" is the first and only complete course for private instruction of all band instruments. Like instruments may be taught in classes. Cornets, trombones, baritones and basses may be taught together. The course is designed to give the student a sound musical background and at the same time provide for the highest degree of interest and motivation. The entire course is correlated to the band oriented sequence.

To make the course both authoritative and practical, most books are co-authored by a national authority on each instrument in collaboration with Fred Weber, perhaps the most widely-known and accepted authority at the student level.

The Belwin "Student Instrumental Course" has three levels: elementary, intermediate, and advanced intermediate. Each level consists of a method and three correlating supplementary books. In addition, a duet book is available for Flute, B♭ Clarinet, E♭ Alto Sax, B♭ Cornet and Trombone. The chart below shows the correlating books available with each part.

The Belwin "STUDENT INSTRUMENTAL COURSE" - A course for individual and class instruction of LIKE instruments, at three levels, for all band instruments.

*EACH BOOK IS COMPLETE IN ITSELF BUT ALL BOOKS ARE CORRELATED WITH EACH OTHER*

**METHOD**
"The Trombone Student"
For individual or Brass class instruction.

*ALTHOUGH EACH BOOK CAN BE USED SEPARATELY, IDEALLY, ALL SUPPLEMENTARY BOOKS SHOULD BE USED AS COMPANION BOOKS WITH THE METHOD*

**STUDIES AND MELODIOUS ETUDES**
Supplementary scales, warm-up and technical drills, musicianship studies and melody-like studies.

**TUNES FOR TECHNIC**
Technical type melodies, variations, and "famous passages" from musical literature — for the development of technical dexterity.

**THE TROMBONE SOLOIST**
Interesting and playable graded easy solo arrangements of famous and well-liked melodies. Also contains 2 Duets, and 1 Trio. Easy piano accompaniments.

**DUETS FOR STUDENTS**
Easy duet arrangements of familiar melodies for early ensemble experience.
Available for: Flute
B♭ Clarinet
Alto Sax
B♭ Cornet
Trombone

# CHART OF TROMBONE POSITIONS

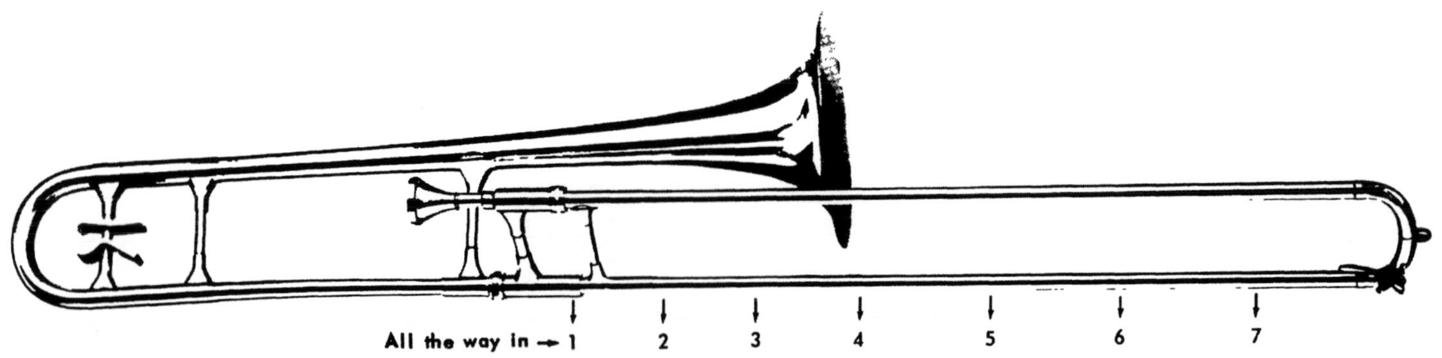


## How To Read The Chart

The number of the position for each note is given in the chart below. See picture above for location of the slide and hand for each position. When two notes are given on the chart (F# and Gb), they are the same tone, and of course, played with the same position.

When two positions for a note are indicated, always use the TOP one unless your teacher tells you otherwise.

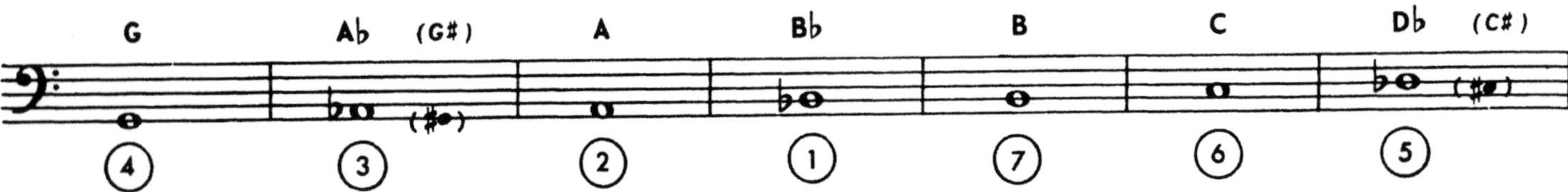


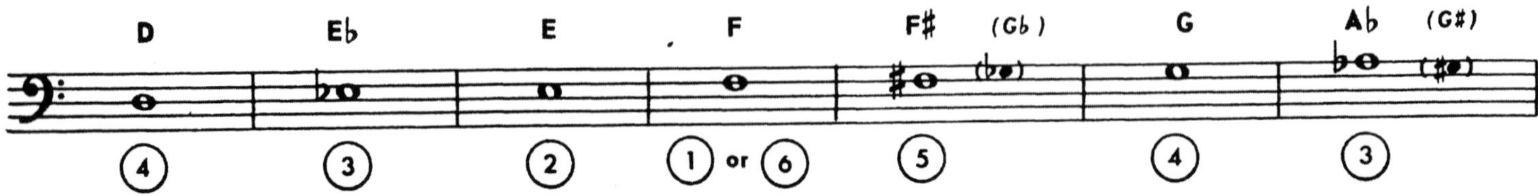


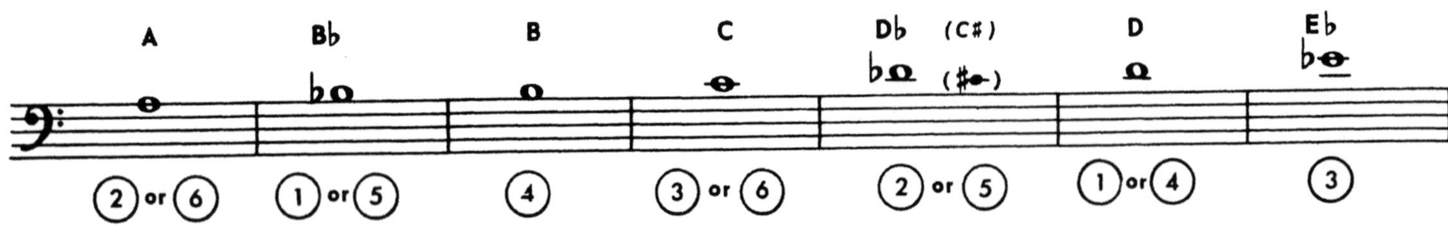


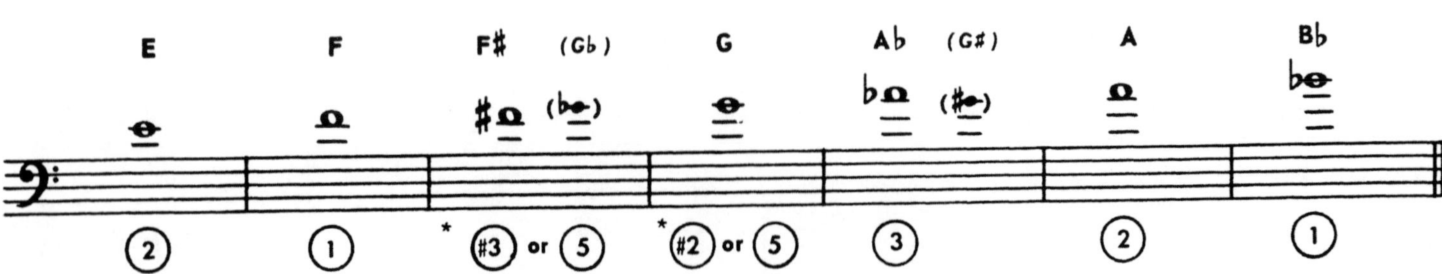


**The # is used to indicate a high position. (The slide should be in a little more than for the regular position.)*

# Getting Started

**On the Trombone we can get several different tones with each slide position, by tightening or loosening the lips.**

**FIRST DO THIS –**

**Play any 1st position tone (slide all the way in). Hold it as long as COMFORTABLE and try to make it as CLEAR and STEADY as possible. Be sure the air goes through the horn in a steady stream.**

**The tone you play will probably be one of THREE tones. We will call them "HIGH", "MIDDLE", and "LOW". Your teacher will tell you which one you are playing.**

**PRACTICE THE THREE NOTES ABOVE**

**Until you can play them with a steady and pleasant sound. Your teacher will tell you which note you are playing.**

**High tones are easier for some beginners while others find the low tones easier to play. Omit the High note or Low note if difficult.**

**NOW DO THIS – If the High notes are easier try the line below.**

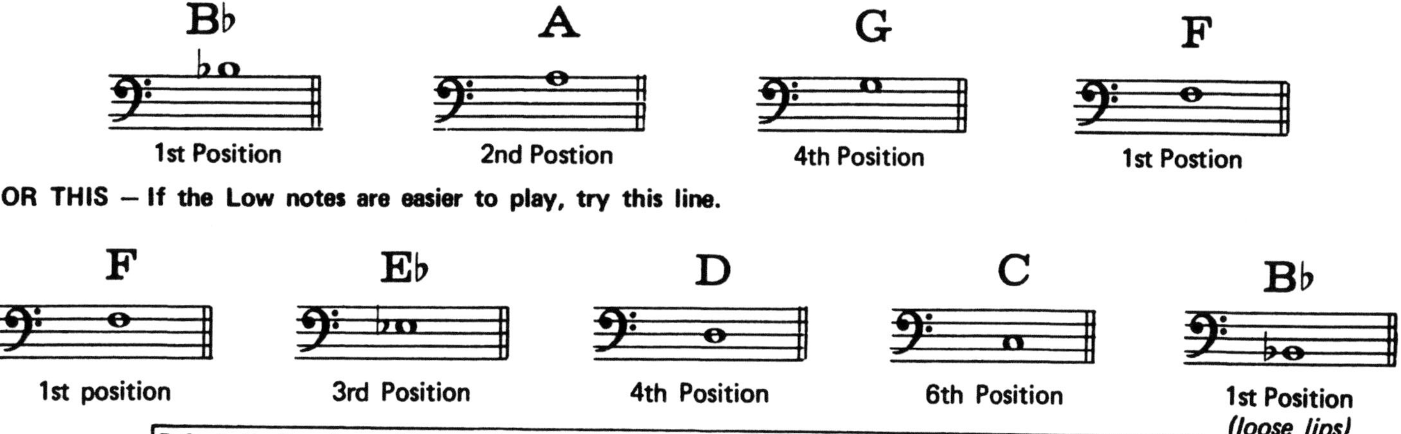


**Refer to the Trombone picture on the top of Page 2, for exact location of the slide for the different positions.**

**If you can play both the HIGH and LOW notes, try playing the line below. Hold each tone as long as comfortable, and be sure each tone is clear and steady.**

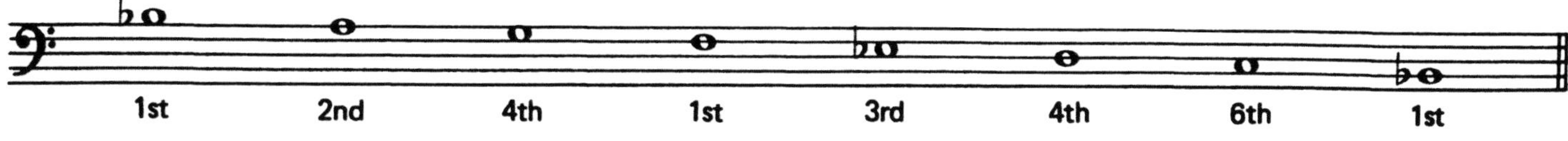

# Reading Music

**You should know the following rudiments before starting to play:**

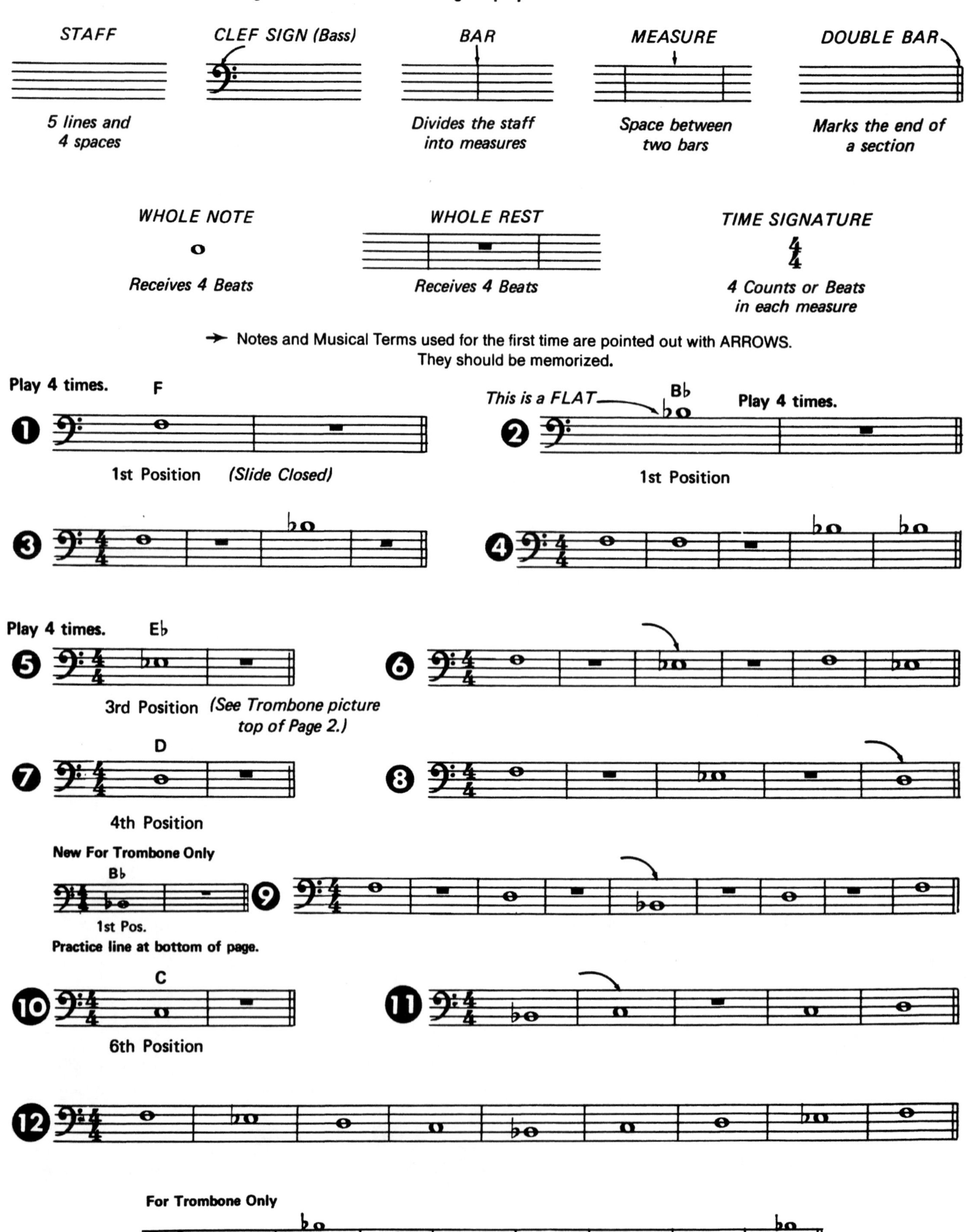

# Lesson 2

## Quarter Notes And Quarter Rests

# Lesson 3

**PUT THE FOLLOWING ON THE STAFF:**

| Whole Note | Quarter Note | A Time Signature | Quarter Rest | Half Note | Half Rest | Tie two Notes |
|---|---|---|---|---|---|---|

# Lesson 4

*KEY SIGNATURES – Up to now, Bb and Eb have been written with a FLAT in front of them. We now start putting the flats at the beginning of the line and call it a Key Signature. In this line we have two flats in the Key Signature. When there are 2 flats in the Key Signature they are always Bb and Eb. This means all Bs and Es in the line are Bb and Eb even though there is no flat in front of them. From this point on always check the key signature before playing a line. LINES 6 and 6A sound exactly the same.

# Special Page For Trombone Only

Up to this point we have "tongued" all notes. From here on, some will be tongued and others will be slurred. A "slur" is indicated by a curved line joining two or more notes. It looks like a "tie" but joins DIFFERENT notes. When two notes are slurred we tongue the first one but play the second either without tonguing or by tonguing softly with a "Doo".

Tonguing and slurring on the trombone is somewhat different than for other instruments because of the slide. The studies and suggestions on this page should help you understand the first principles of proper trombone tonguing and slurring. Practice this page carefully and follow your teacher's suggestions because proper tonguing is very important on the trombone.

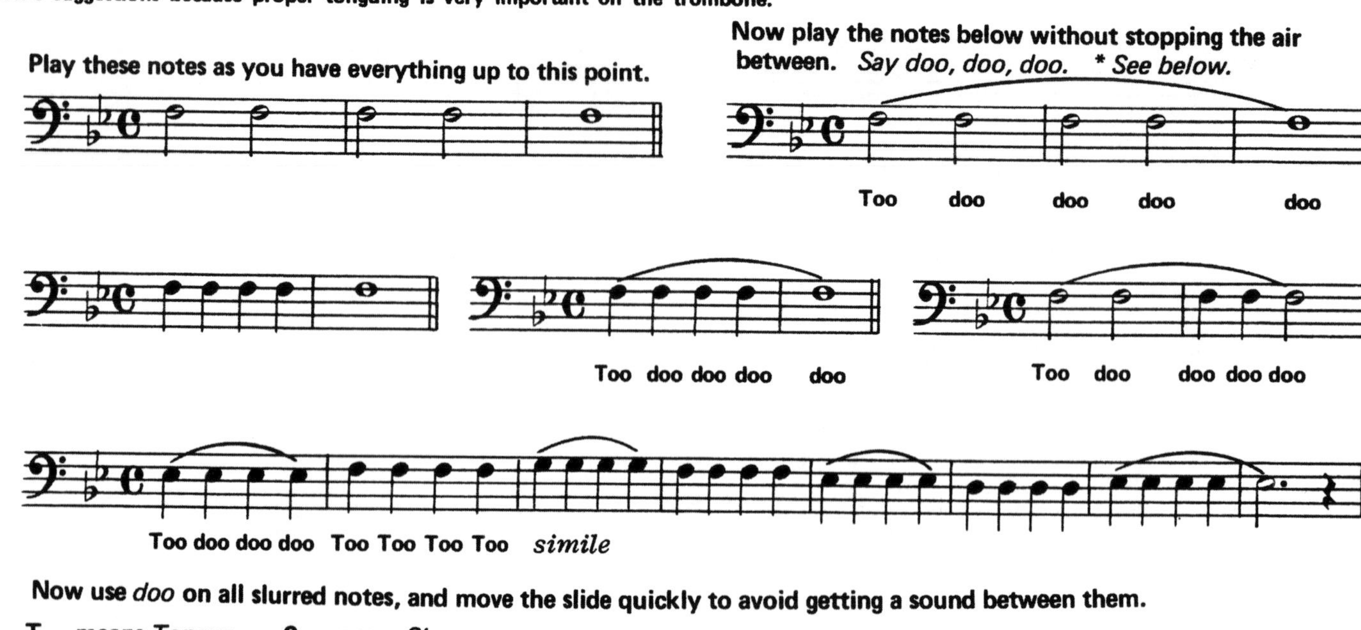
Play these notes as you have everything up to this point.
Now play the notes below without stopping the air between. *Say doo, doo, doo.* * *See below.*
Too doo doo doo doo
Too doo doo doo doo
Too doo doo doo doo
Too doo doo doo Too Too Too Too *simile*
Now use *doo* on all slurred notes, and move the slide quickly to avoid getting a sound between them.
T – *means Tongue* S – *means Slur*

T S T S T S T T T
T S T S T T S T S T

Now use *doo* on all notes below, and move slide quickly to avoid getting a sound between the notes.

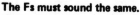

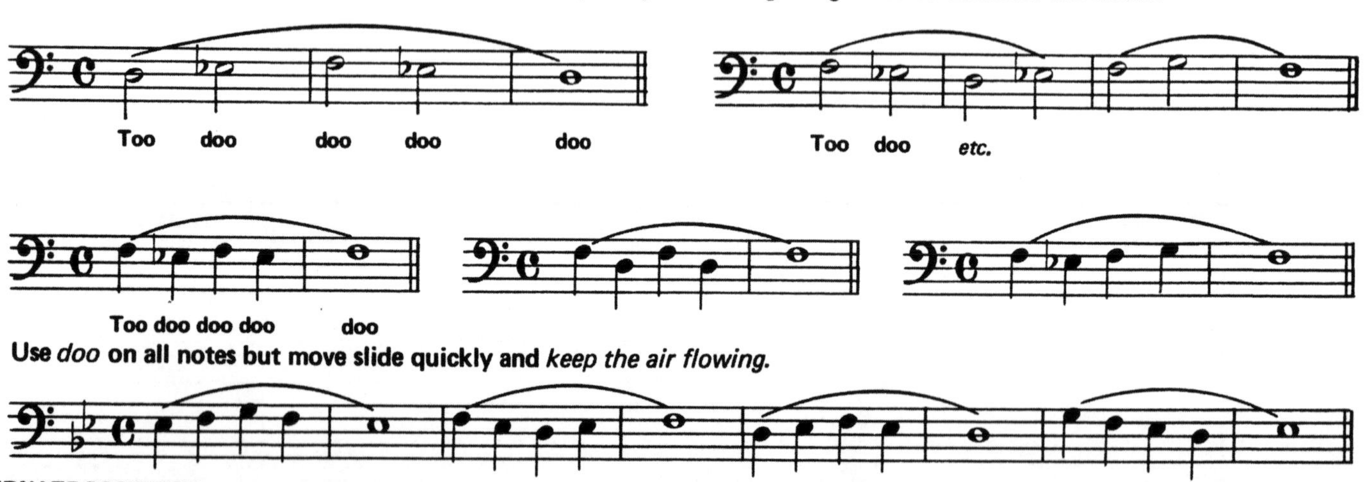
Too doo doo doo doo
Too doo *etc.*
Too doo doo doo doo
Use *doo* on all notes but move slide quickly and *keep the air flowing.*

**ALTERNATE POSITIONS**

Some notes on the trombone can be played in more than one position. These additional positions are called *"Alternate Positions"*. It is very important to learn HOW and WHEN to use these alternate positions because it leads to faster and smoother playing as you progress. They are absolutely essential in more advanced trombone playing. Additional information on alternate positions will be given where appropriate.

The Fs must sound the same.

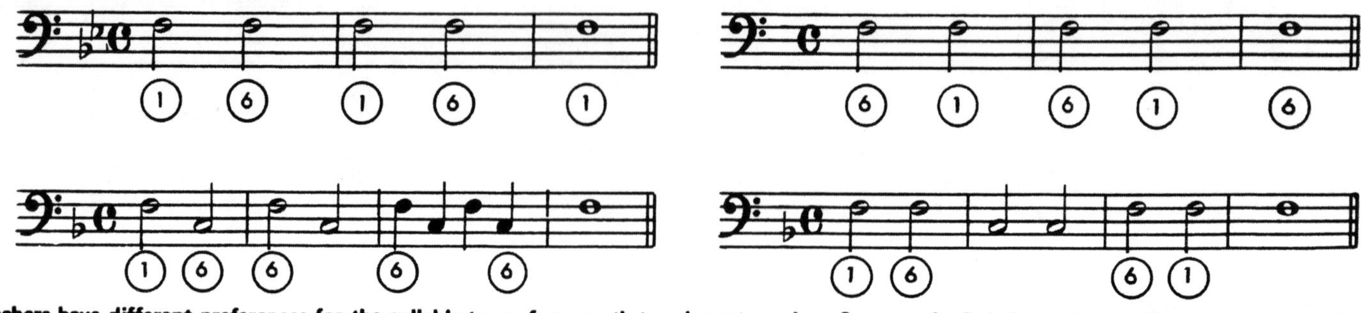
1 6 1 6 1
6 1 6 1 6
1 6 6 6 6
1 6 6 1

* Teachers have different preferences for the syllable to use for smooth trombone tonguing. Some prefer Dah, loo, rah, etc. Follow your teacher's preference.

# Lesson 5

SLUR - Tongue the first note of each slur only. Ask your teacher to explain.
1
2
A Flatted note sounds ½ step lower than the natural or regular note.
Ab
3
Also Ab (*See below)
* A Flat or Sharp remains in effect throughout the entire measure.
Go Tell Aunt Rhode
4
KEY SIGNATURE – see note below*
5
In the piece above, name and circle the three notes that are to be flatted ___ ___ ___ .
6
7
Also Ab
Skips
8
What is the name of the basic tune?
Crazy Counting
9
2/4 TIME - 2 counts in each measure.
March Trio
10
Circle all notes that are flatted.
Also Ab
* When there are three flats, the third flat is always Ab and the Key is Eb. This means the piece is based on the Eb Scale and all Bs, Es and As are flatted.
1 Put names of notes in squares above staff.
2 Put position number in circle below staff.

# Lesson 6

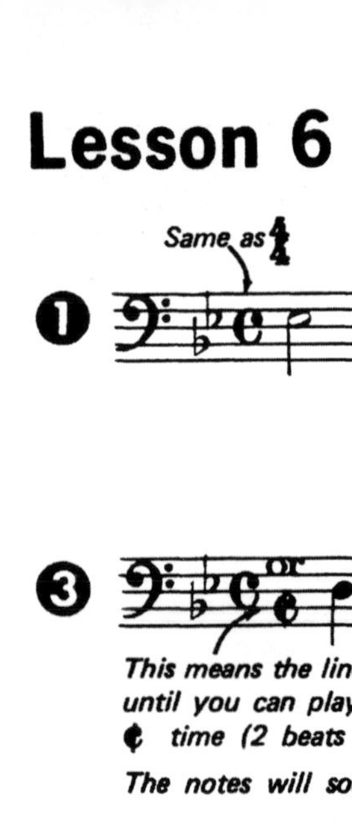


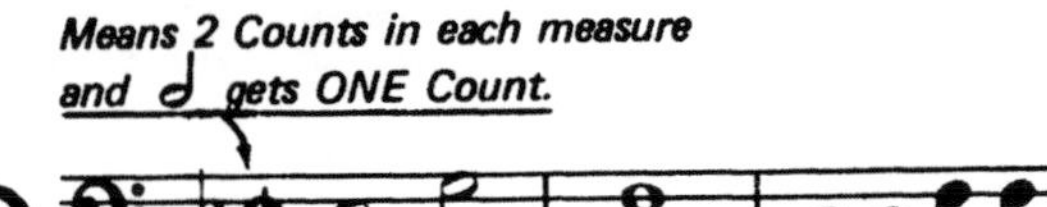


## Jingle Bells

This means the line may be played either in C or ¢ time. Practice the line in C time until you can play it well, then play the notes AT THE SAME SPEED but TAP in ¢ time (2 beats per measure).

The notes will sound the same, only the TAPPING will be different.

Write counting under notes, then play.

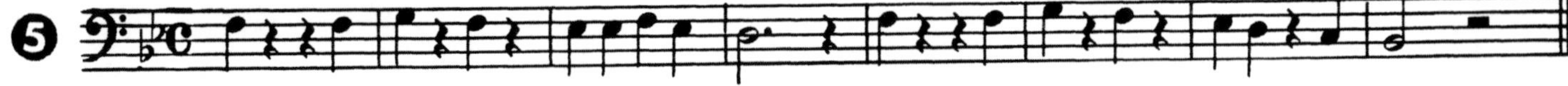


ALWAYS check Key Signature and Time Signature before playing line or piece.

Circle all notes that are flatted.

## Two Tune Duet

*Ask your teacher if he wants you to practice the scale below at this time.*

**The B♭ SCALE is first used in Lesson 8 on Page 12, however, a little exploratory practice on this scale might be helpful at this time.**

Lesson 7
You are now ready to begin the companion books, STUDIES AND MELODIOUS ETUDES and TUNES FOR TECHNIC, correlated with the Method as part of the BELWIN STUDENT INSTRUMENTAL COURSE.
Low A
1
Cuckoo Waltz
Repeat preceeding measure
2
3
4
Speed Drill
5
Play 4 times and work for speed.
Hold each note as long as possible.
6
Listen carefully to each tone.
A Skip Around Song
7
Count 3 1 2 3
Fine
(Finish)
D. C. al Fine
(Go Back to Beginning and Play to Fine.)
8
Old MacDonald's Duet
Write counting under each line before playing.
9
Both lines played together as a Duet will sound the complete melody. One person can also play both lines for the melody.
On the staff below, write the note receiving the number of counts called for (in 4/4 time).
4 2 1 3 1 2 4 2 3 4 2 1 3 4 2 3 1

# Our First Solo

Trombone

*Solo*

1 2

Piano Accompaniment

1 2

On the top staff is a series of notes and rests. You are to rewrite this line on the bottom staff changing notes to rests of the same time value and rests to notes of the same time value.

# Lesson 8

♮ NATURAL - cancels the effect of a Flat or Sharp.
To remind you the note isn't A♭.
A♮
B♭
REVIEW
1
Notice - 2 Flats
FOR TROMBONE ONLY
2
3
4
Notice - 3 Flats
To remind you
5
March
To remind you
6
Speed Drill
Work out carefully, then try for speed.
7
Also played slurred.
Marines' Hymn
PICK UP NOTES
8
Count
Fine
D. C. al Fine
1 Put in the Bar Lines.
2 Write counting under notes.

# Lesson 9

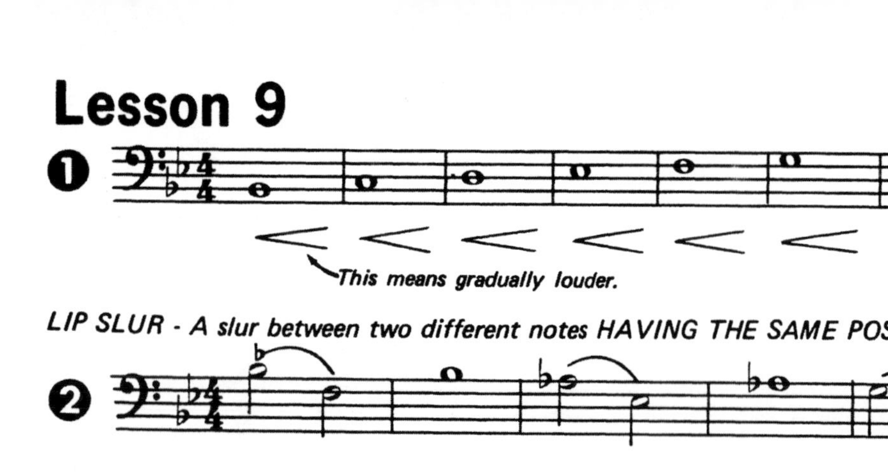
This means gradually louder.
Apply to scale.

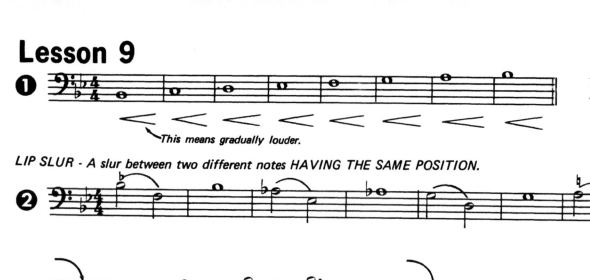

*LIP SLUR - A slur between two different notes HAVING THE SAME POSITION.*

## Grandfather's Clock

*Fine*
*(Finish)*

*D. C. al Fine*

## Caisson March

**Write a T below the ties and an S below the slurs.**

Tongue one measure in regular manner, the next tongue using *doo.*

Play these slurs using *doo* as you have until now.

Now play the slurs with *NO* tongue except at the beginning of each slur.

Use *NO* tongue when slide stays in same position and you change notes. When you move the slide, tongue with *doo.*

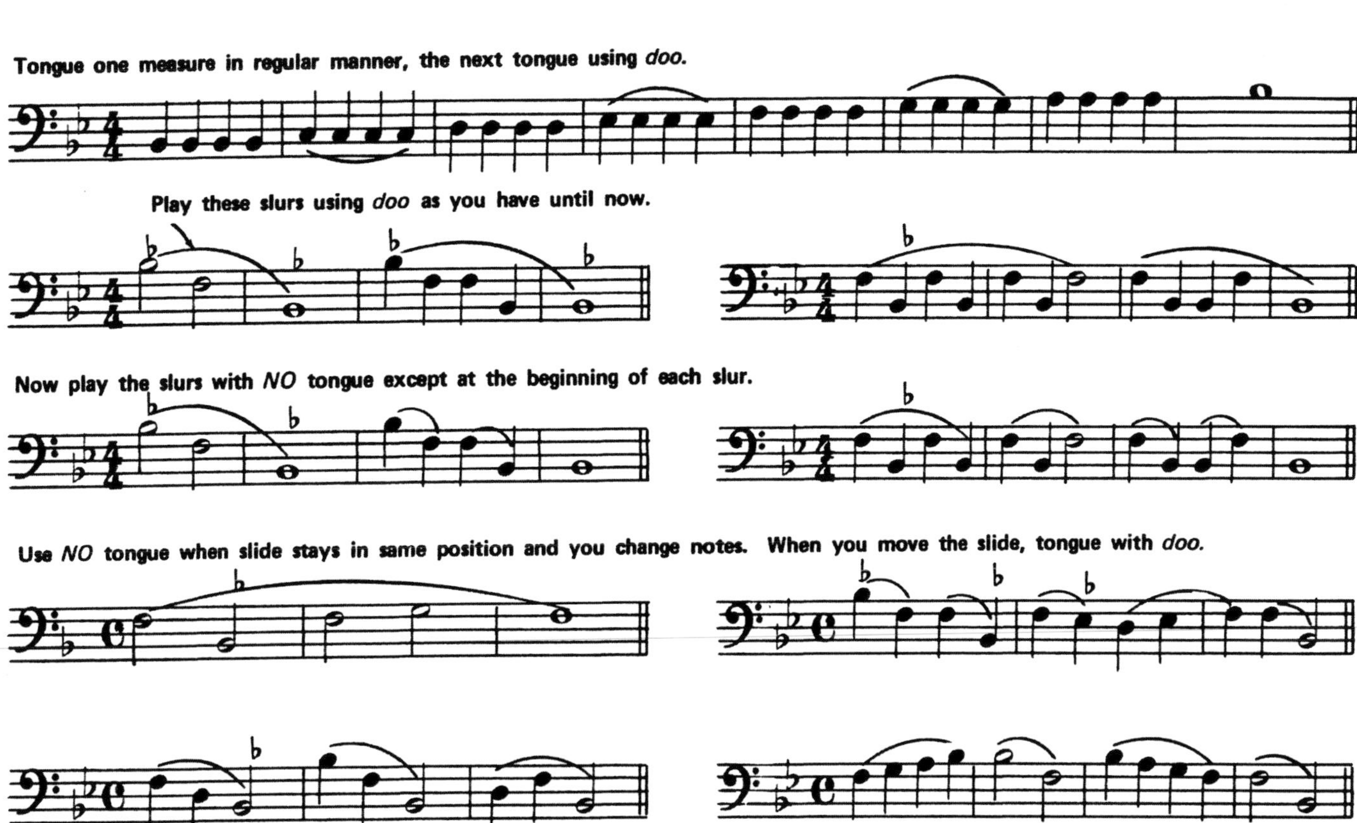

## Flat Keys

On the trombone we usually learn some of the *"Flat"* keys and scales first. This is because they are easier to play and the Young Band plays to a large extent in these keys (F, B♭, and A♭). You must be careful not to mix the "flats" and "naturals", especially E and A in the beginning.

The three lines below should help you distinguish clearly A, A♭, and A♮, and how they are affected by the Key Signature. Study them carefully.

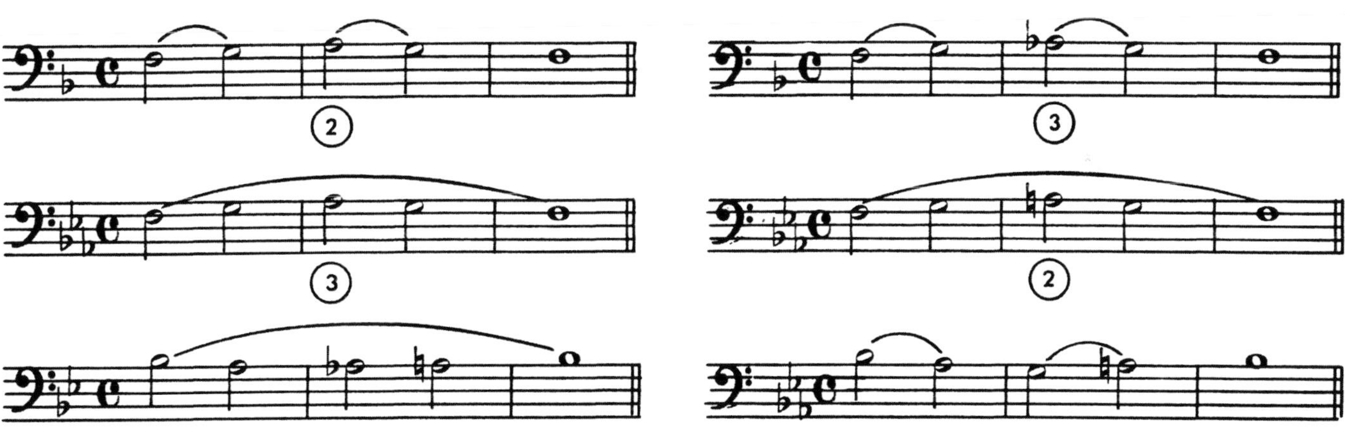

## Alternate Position Studies

Some notes can be played in more than one position.

It is sometimes easier to use an alternate position because it doesn't require as much slide movement.

Most of the time F (4th line) is played 1st position but there are times, usually when going between F and 2nd space C, when there is an advantage in playing F in 6th position. The lines below will point this out.

In the line below, the student should decide which position is most logical.

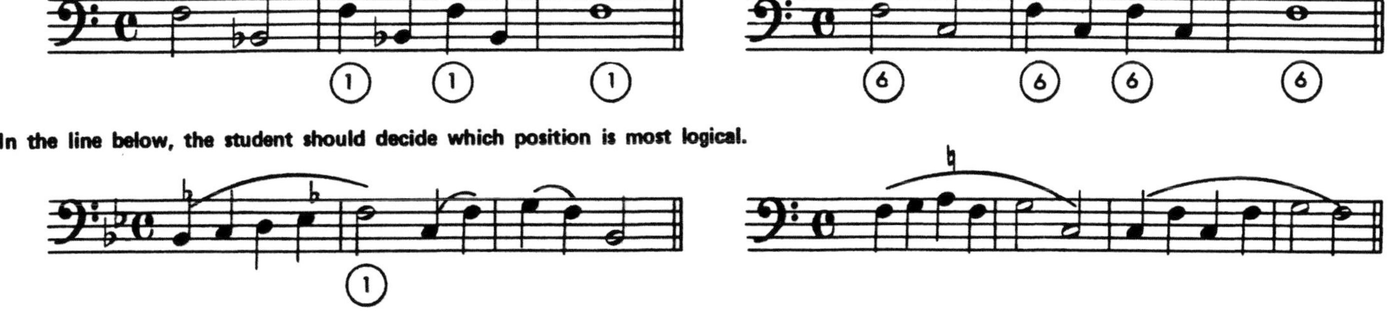

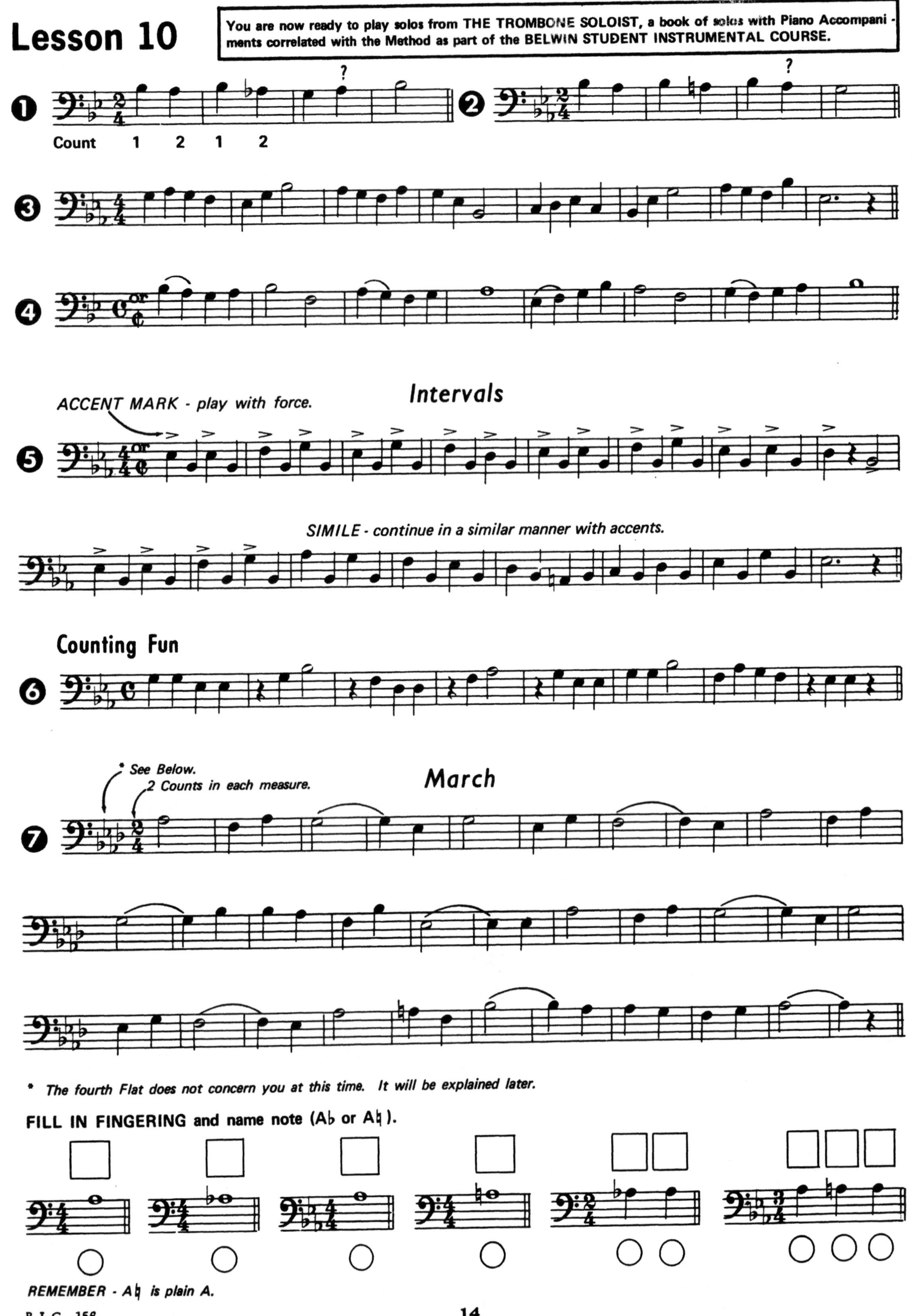
Lesson 10
You are now ready to play solos from THE TROMBONE SOLOIST, a book of solos with Piano Accompaniments correlated with the Method as part of the BELWIN STUDENT INSTRUMENTAL COURSE.
Count 1 2 1 2
ACCENT MARK - play with force.
Intervals
SIMILE - continue in a similar manner with accents.
Counting Fun
* See Below.
2 Counts in each measure.
March
* The fourth Flat does not concern you at this time. It will be explained later.
FILL IN FINGERING and name note (A♭ or A♮).
REMEMBER - A♮ is plain A.

# Lesson 11

A Natural cancels a Flat (or sharp).
E
②
Church Song
This is written in the Key of B♭ to emphasize E♮ using a ♮ sign. See Number 5 for "Church Song" written in Key of F as it should be written.
There is only ONE Flat.
All E's are played E natural - (just plain E).
2
2 Flats
3
To remind you the note isn't E♭
1
2
Compare with No. 2. Notice how much easier it looks when written in Key of F and ♮ sign isn't necessary.
*See below.
?
?
Bicycle Built For Two
Double Note Duet
Student (or Teacher)
Teacher (or Student)

*When we have 1 Flat in the Key Signature, it is always B♭ and the Key is F. It means the piece is based on the scale of F. You must be careful to play E (2nd position) instead of E♭ (3rd position).

# Lesson 12

You are now ready for DUETS FOR STUDENTS, a book of easy duet arrangements of familiar melodies coordinated with the BELWIN STUDENT INSTRUMENTAL COURSE.

Circle the notes that are to be flatted.

Circle the notes that are to be flatted.

Circle all Es. What position do we use for E in this line?

## Speed Drill

Work out carefully - then try for speed.

## March Theme

# Lesson 13

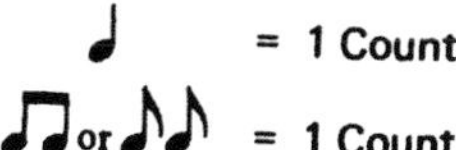

Play Number 1 first in 4/4 time - then in Cut ( ¢ ) Time. Then play Number 2 as written. Compare Number 1 played in ¢ time with Number 2 played in eighth notes.

Your teacher will show you his favorite way of counting eithth notes.

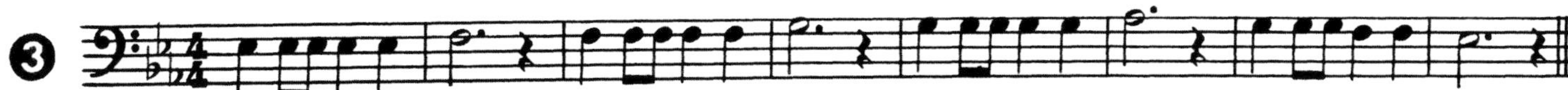

*If the foot-tapping method of counting is used make sure the foot comes UP (Up beat) in EXACTLY the MIDDLE of the BEAT.*

## Intervals

Play slowly and separate tones. DO NOT STOP tone with the tongue.

## Chromatics

Also play slurred.

## Melody Fun

Play 3 times. The first time play the entire melody. 2nd time - omit all notes marked with ★ and substitute a rest. 3rd time - omit all notes marked ★ and + and substitute quarter rests.

# Special Page For Trombone Only

Play these slurs with *doo* as you have until now.

Now play the slurs with NO tongue, except at the beginning of each slur.

On the 2 lines below, use *doo*, only when you move the slide; otherwise do not tongue except at the beginning of each slur.

The 3 lines below should help you distinguish clearly between E, E♭, and E♮ and how they are affected by the key signature. Study them carefully.

## E♭ And E♮

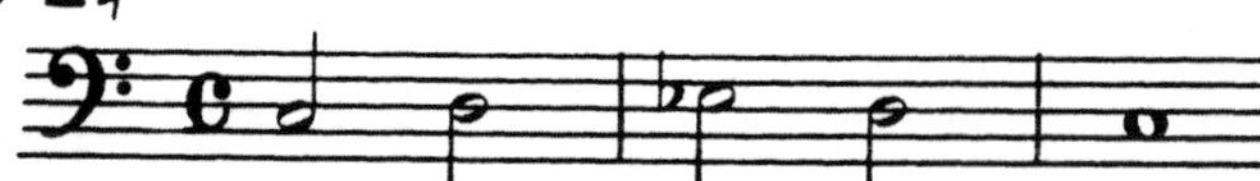

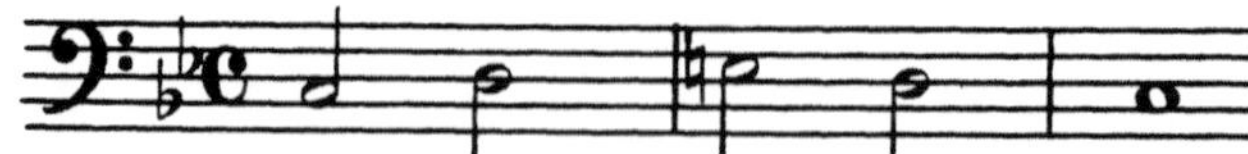

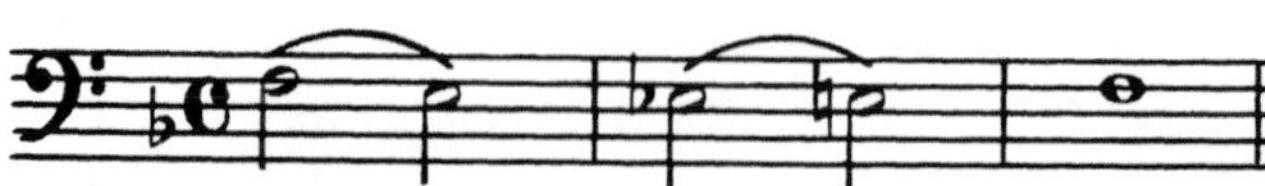

## High Notes

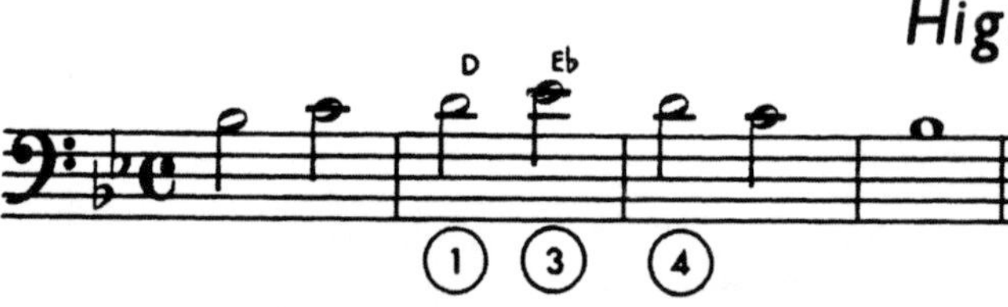

D is usually played 1st position but it can be played in the 4th position. It is usually played 4th position when between two 3rd position notes such as high C and E♭ or C and C or E♭ and E♭.

First play using your regular position for F, then play using positions as marked. Which is easier?

It may seem a little tricky to learn these alternate positions and when to use them, but when you have mastered their use your playing will become much easier and you will be able to play faster.

# Lesson 14

is intended to picture a well played tone that doesn't wave and stays on exactly the same pitch.
1
Avoid tones of the types pictured below.
ⓐ A "Scooped" attack.
ⓑ A wavy Tone.
ⓒ Attack not clean.
ⓓ A Tone that goes flat.
ⓔ (1) Accented tongue release.
(2) Over-accented attack.
(1)
(2)
2
Count 1 2 3 + 4
⑥ ①
3
This Old Man
4
There's A Hole In The Bucket
5
Count 3 + 1
⑥ ⑥ ⑥ ⑥ ① ⑥ ⑥ ①
When The Saints Go Marching In
Pick Up Notes
6
Count 4/4 2 3 4 1
¢ + 2 + 1
Write the counting under the measures below.
1 2 3 4

# Lesson 15

This means gradually softer.
LIP SLURS - Practice slurring two ways (TOP and BOTTOM MARKINGS).
Chromatics
Speed Drill
Work out slowly, then try for speed.
Billy Boy
Counting Fun
What tune is this study based on?

# Lesson 16

Tune in KEY OF B♭ ( 2 Flats )
1
or
Same Tune in KEY OF E♭ ( 3 Flats )
2
or
Same Tune in KEY OF F ( 1 Flat )
3
or
Scale Study in KEY OF B♭
4
or
Scale Study in KEY OF F
5
or
Scale Study in KEY OF E♭
6
or
Because You're You
7
Low B♮
7
7
6
Grandfather's Clock
8
Count 2 1 2 + etc.
6
Fine
6
D.C. al Fine
In the measures below is the second note HIGHER; LOWER; or the SAME as the first note? Use H, L, and S.
H

# Lesson 17

𝄾 EIGHTH REST - Same value as eighth note (♪).
Staccato – means short or separated.
1
etc.
NEVER stop the tone with the tongue.
2
Andante From The Surprise Symphony
HAYDN
3
Work out carefully, then try for speed.
The Name Of This Key Is____?
4
Swing High March
C#
5
Trio

# Lesson 18

Work for a steady tone (as pictured) with no changes of pitch.
1
etc.
Enharmonic Tones
F♯ (G♭)
same sound
2
5
3
etc.
Intervals
simile
4
etc.
The Name Of This Key Is____?
Work out carefully, then try for speed.
or
5
Mighty 'Lak A Rose
6
1
2

# Lesson 19

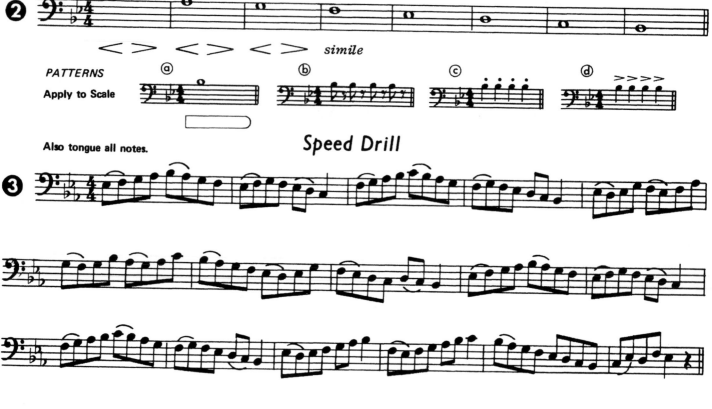

Accent Mark

❶

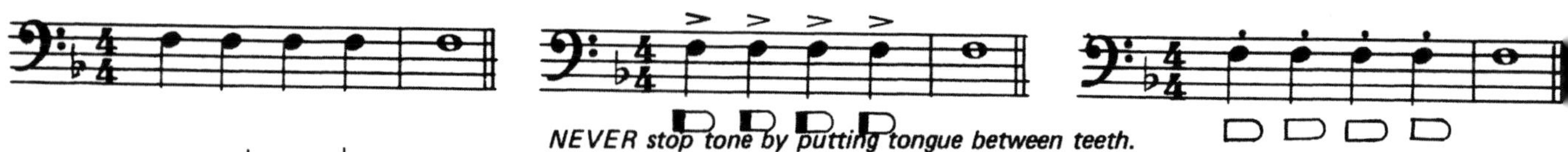

NEVER stop tone by putting tongue between teeth.

NOTICE - both ♩> and ♩. notes are separated. ♩> is accented; ♩. is not accented.

❷

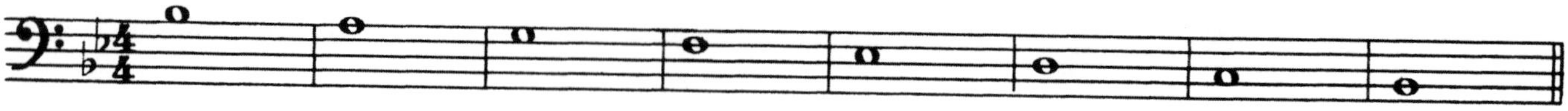

< > < > < > *simile*

PATTERNS
Apply to Scale

ⓐ ⓑ ⓒ ⓓ

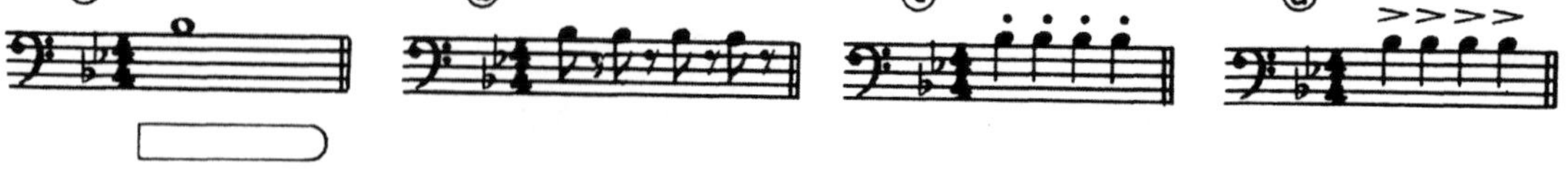

Also tongue all notes.

## Speed Drill

❸

## Counting Fun

❹

## Mexican Clapping Song

❺

## The Blue Tail Fly

❻

# Lesson 20

1
Apply each pattern to entire scale in line 1.
PATTERNS
ⓐ
ⓑ
ⓒ
ⓓ
ff mf p
D (C♯)
2
same
DOTTED QUARTER NOTE
3
The author suggests that you tap twice on the dotted quarter notes ( ♩. ). The eighth note ( ♪ ) comes midway between the 2nd and 3rd taps, (on the up-beat after 2).
America
4
p Stands for PIANO and means play softly.
5
Count 1 2 + 3
Home On The Range
6
f Stands for FORTE and means play loudly.
Michael Row The Boat
7
Count 3 4 1 2 + 3 4
What KEY is this?________
What KEY?________
What KEY?________

# Lesson 21

## A Page of Counting Fun

*Carnival Of Venice*

Theme And Nine Variations

# Lesson 22

1
etc.
Play staccato 1st time and legato 2nd time. LEGATO means very smooth - use a soft tongue stroke with NO separation of notes.
2
Db
②
When there are 4 flats in the Key Signature — —
ALL Bs, Es, As, and Ds in any octave are flatted.
REVIEW
3
Db
⑤
4
or
Play tongued first, then play slurred as marked.
Work out carefully, then try for speed.
Speed Drill
5
or
Also tongue each note.
College Song
6
mp
Stands for MEZZO PIANO and means to play moderately soft.
Over The Waves
7
⑤
mf
Stands for MEZZO FORTE and means to play moderately loud.
③
Same as Ab

# Lesson 23

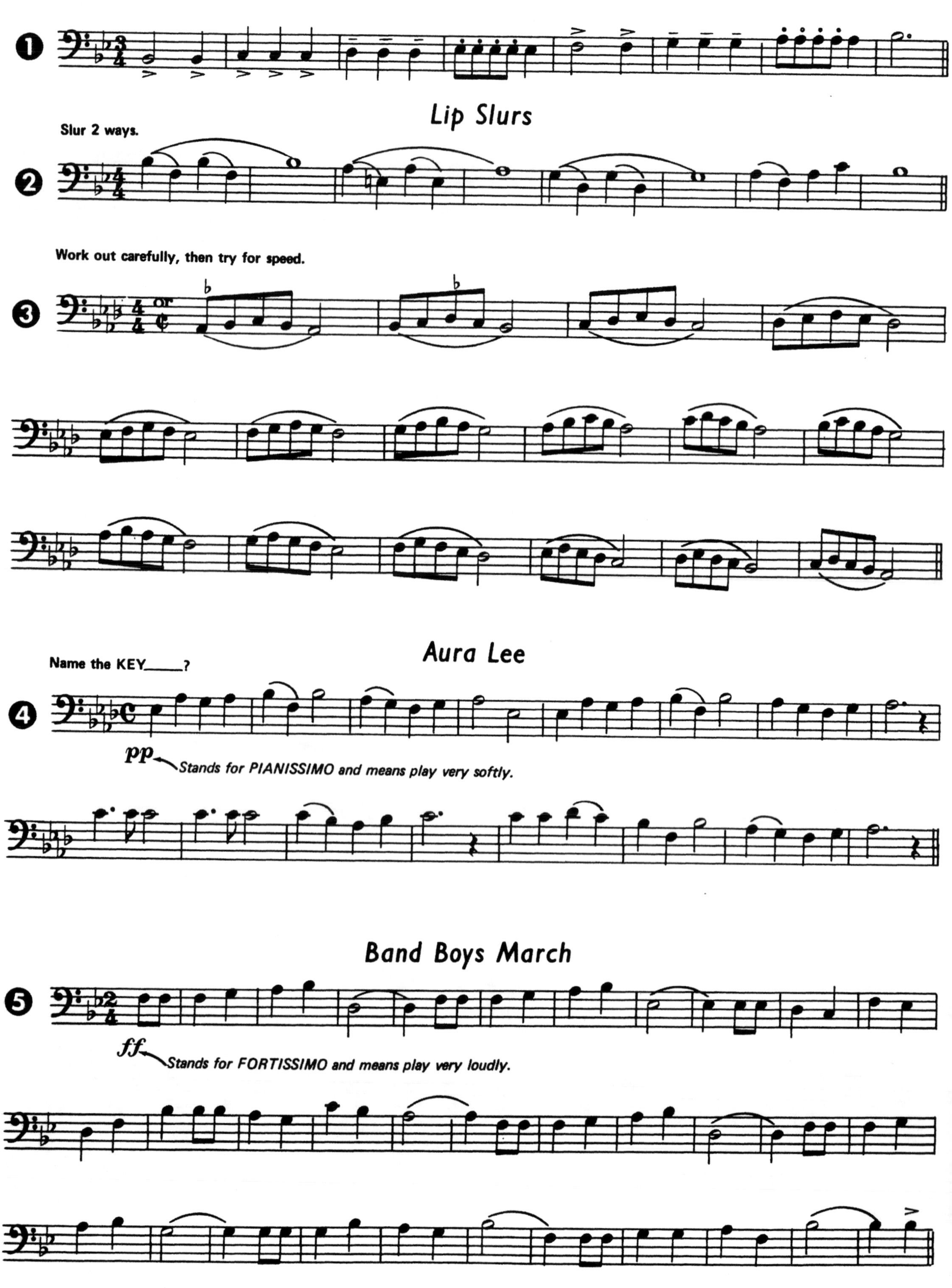

1
Lip Slurs
Slur 2 ways.
2
Work out carefully, then try for speed.
3
or
Aura Lee
Name the KEY_____?
4
pp
Stands for PIANISSIMO and means play very softly.
Band Boys March
5
ff
Stands for FORTISSIMO and means play very loudly.

# Lesson 24

The name of this KEY is_______?
The name of this KEY is_______?
The name of this KEY is_______?
The name of this KEY is_______?
Chromatic Review
Counting Review
Articulation Review

# Lesson 25

ff f mp pp pp p f ff
See next line.
♪ - EIGHTH NOTE receives ONE count.
3/8 TIME - 3 counts to each measure.
♪ - 1 Count; ♩ - 2 Counts; ♩. - 3 Counts.
KEY of____?
The Man On The Flying Trapeze
mf
6
6
Sweet Betsy From Pike
Same tempo ♪ = ♩
mp
Don't stop

# Lesson 26

Chromatic Scale
6/8 Time
6/8 TIME is played exactly like 3/8 Time except there are 6 Counts in each measure. (♩. = 6 Counts)
Glow Worm
mp
ALWAYS check Key Signature and Time Signature before playing a line or piece.
America The Beautiful
f

# Lesson 27

1
5
5
2
Separate each note.
simile
3
4
6
My Wild Irish Rose
4
p
Yankee Doodle Boy
5
ff
6
6
6

# Lesson 28

Sixteenth Notes
1
2
4
– receives 1 Count
– receive 1 Count
– receive 1 Count
Count 1 + 2
1 + 2 +
If the foot-tapping method of counting is used make sure the foot comes UP (Up beat) in EXACTLY the MIDDLE of the BEAT.
Jig
mf
Bill Bailey, Won't You Please Come Home

# Lesson 29

D
①
B♮
④
William Tell Theme
E♭
③
Count
+
1
f
Variations On Skip To M'Lou
mp
American Patrol
March tempo
f
⑥

# esson 30

1
2
3
Dinah
4
f
6
Bugle Call
Use 6th position throughout.
Play using different positions (3rd position throughout, etc.).
5
mf

# Lesson 31

If slurring is difficult, tongue each note softly (*doo*).

❶ Name notes. ❷ Mark positions.

* *When there is no Flat (or Sharp), the Key is C. YOU MUST BE CAREFUL not to flat Bs and Es. They are natural.*

# Lesson 32

* KEY SIGNATURE - (See note below)
5
Apply these rhythms to the Scale.
Circle all flatted notes.
6
Brahm's Lullaby
PHRASE MARK - Discuss phrasing with your teacher.
p
Play smoothly in a singing style.

* When there are five flats, the fifth flat is always G♭ and the Key is D♭. This means the piece is based on the D♭ Scale and all Bs, Es, As, Ds and Gs are flatted.

# Basic Technic

# Basic Technic

## Lip Slurs

Practice as assigned by your Teacher.

A
A1
A2
A3
A4
Use the above slide positions on Pattern A
Intervals
Fourths
simile
Play slowly and separate each tone.
simile
Octaves
Play slowly and separate each tone.
simile

B.I.C. 156

# Range Builders

## Special Page For Trombone Only

## *High Notes And Alternate D*

**D above the staff is usually played in 1st position but frequently it is best to play it in 4th position. It is usually played in 4th position when it comes between C and E♭; C and C; or E♭ and E♭. As a general rule, it is best to play it in the closest position or the position that requires the least slide movement.**

**On the bottom line the student should decide which is the proper position for high D.**

# Basic Technic

**The Patterns below provide for unlimited scale practice in the 7 most common band keys.**

*Start with ANY line and play through the entire pattern without stopping. Return to the STARTING LINE and play to where the END is marked. You must keep the KEY SIGNATURE of the STARTING LINE THROUGHOUT the entire pattern.*

# Speed Tests

Name the notes. Work for speed. Each test should be completed in 1 minute and 15 seconds or less.

*Completed in ____ Seconds.*

SPEED TEST 1

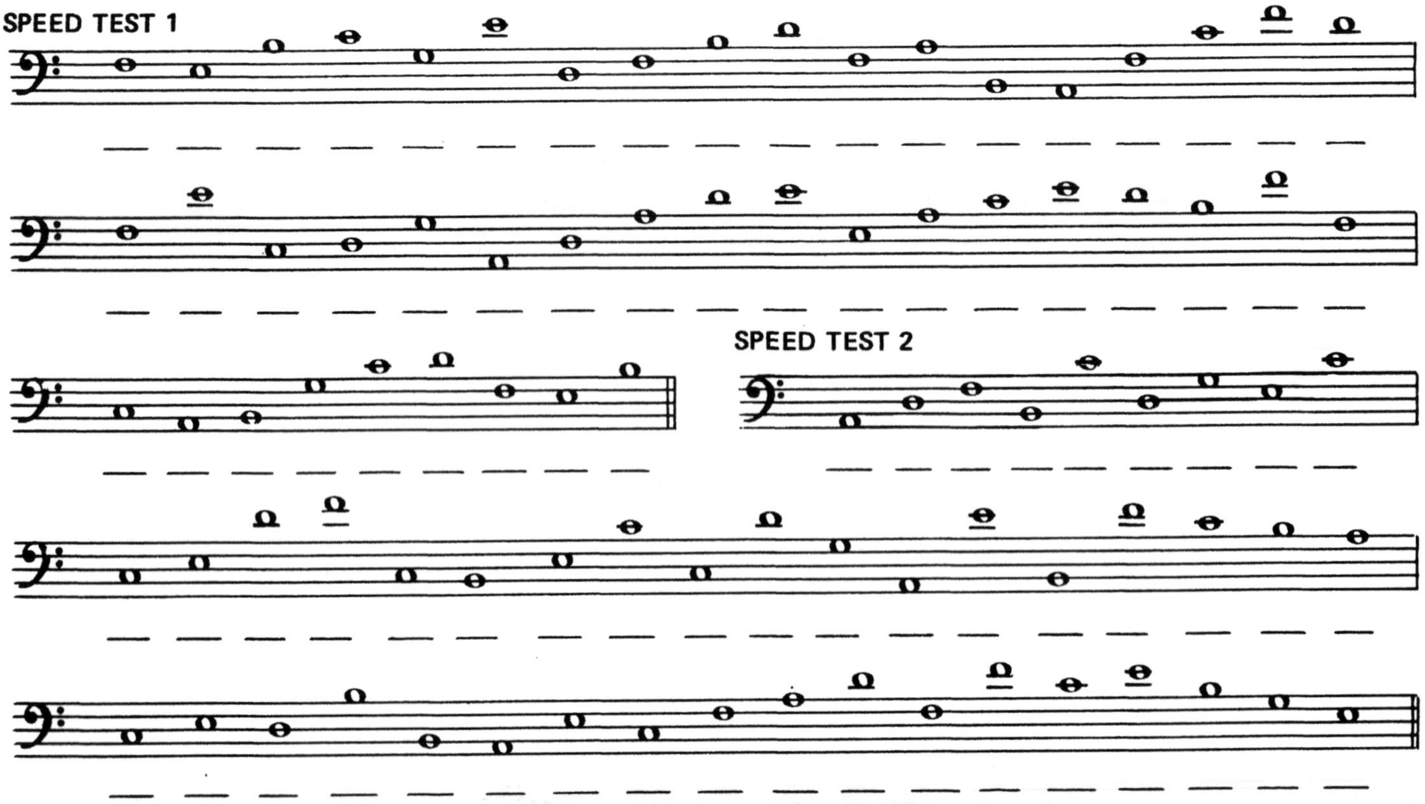

SPEED TEST 2

# Home Practice Record

| Week | Mon. | Tues. | Wed. | Thurs. | Fri. | Sat. | Total | Parent's Signature | Week | Mon. | Tues. | Wed. | Thurs. | Fri. | Sat. | Total | Parent's Signature |
|---|---|---|---|---|---|---|---|---|---|---|---|---|---|---|---|---|---|
| 1 | | | | | | | | | 21 | | | | | | | | |
| 2 | | | | | | | | | 22 | | | | | | | | |
| 3 | | | | | | | | | 23 | | | | | | | | |
| 4 | | | | | | | | | 24 | | | | | | | | |
| 5 | | | | | | | | | 25 | | | | | | | | |
| 6 | | | | | | | | | 26 | | | | | | | | |
| 7 | | | | | | | | | 27 | | | | | | | | |
| 8 | | | | | | | | | 28 | | | | | | | | |
| 9 | | | | | | | | | 29 | | | | | | | | |
| 10 | | | | | | | | | 30 | | | | | | | | |
| 11 | | | | | | | | | 31 | | | | | | | | |
| 12 | | | | | | | | | 32 | | | | | | | | |
| 13 | | | | | | | | | 33 | | | | | | | | |
| 14 | | | | | | | | | 34 | | | | | | | | |
| 15 | | | | | | | | | 35 | | | | | | | | |
| 16 | | | | | | | | | 36 | | | | | | | | |
| 17 | | | | | | | | | 37 | | | | | | | | |
| 18 | | | | | | | | | 38 | | | | | | | | |
| 19 | | | | | | | | | 39 | | | | | | | | |
| 20 | | | | | | | | | 40 | | | | | | | | |